D1302441

U.S. HOLOCAUST MEMORIAL MUSEUM

HISTORIC LANDMARKS

Jason Cooper

The Rourke Book Company, Inc.
Vero Beach, Florida 32964

PHOTO CREDITS:
© Alan Gilbert: title page, page 21 ; © U.S. Holocaust Memorial Museum: cover, pages 7 & 17 photos by Lisa Berg; pages 4, 12, 13, 15 photos by Max Reid; pages 8 & 18 photos by Edward Owen; page 10 photo by Arnold Kramer

PRODUCED & DESIGNED by East Coast Studios
eastcoaststudios.com

EDITORIAL SERVICES:
Janice L. Smith for Penworthy Learning Systems

Library of Congress Cataloging-in-Publication Data

Cooper, Jason, 1942-
    U.S. Holocaust Memorial Museum / Jason Cooper.
        p. cm. — (Historic Landmarks)
    Includes index.
    ISBN 1-55916-330-5
    1. United States Holocaust Memorial Museum—Juvenile literature.
2. Holocaust, Jewish (1939-1945)—Juvenile literature. [1. United States
Holocaust Memorial Museum. 2. Holocaust, Jewish (1939-1945) 3. Museums.]
I. Title: US Holocaust Memorial Museum. II. Title.

D804.175 .W373 2000
940.53'074753—dc21
                                                    00–030377

Printed in the USA

TABLE OF CONTENTS

THE U.S. HOLOCAUST MEMORIAL MUSEUM

The United States Holocaust Memorial Museum in Washington, D.C., opened in 1993 to serve many purposes.

The museum is a memorial to millions of people who died in the **Holocaust** (HAH luh kahst) during World War II (1939-1945). The United States has hundreds of memorials. This one is different. It remembers people who weren't Americans and who did not **perish** (PAIR ish) on American soil. They died in Europe, at the hands of **Nazi** (NAHT see) Germany.

The U.S. Congress acted to establish the U.S. Holocaust Memorial Museum in Washington, D.C. This is the 15th Street/Eisenhower Plaza entry.

The museum is also a place to study and think about the Holocaust. No one can visit the museum and not wonder: How? Why?

The museum has collected books, films, paintings, letters, and **artifacts** (AHR teh fakts), or objects, about the Holocaust. Together, these materials reveal some of the horror and tragedy of the Holocaust.

Visitors enter the exhibit especially for children, called "Daniel's Story."

THE HOLOCAUST

You can't know why there is a National Holocaust Museum, of course, without knowing something about the Holocaust itself. The Holocaust was the mass murder of 12 million people. Six million people were Jews who lived in Europe. Among other groups targeted by the Nazis were Gypsies, Poles, Slavs, and Russian prisoners of war.

At the Museum, the shoes of Holocaust victims are grim, silent reminders of the victims who wore them.

SCHOOL

Germany and the Nazi party were under the control of Adolph Hitler from 1933 until 1945. In April, 1945, Hitler killed himself as Germany's war machine failed.

Hitler believed the Germans to be a **superior** (soo PEER ee ur) race of people. Hitler felt special hatred toward Jewish people. He blamed German Jews for Germany's defeat in World War I (1914-1918). He also blamed them for the lack of jobs in Germany.

This railroad car is on the third floor of the Museum. It is one of several kinds of freight cars that were used to take Jews to concentration camps and crowded city buildings called ghettos.

*Like the Nazi death camps, the Museum's
Hall of Witness is simple and spare in design.*

Visitors are seen in a second floor view of the Museum's Hall of Remembrance.

Before World War II began, the Nazis took away Jewish rights and property. By 1939, about half the Jews in Germany had fled. Many who remained in Europe, however, were later caught by the Nazis.

In January, 1942, the Nazi leaders of Germany made the widespread murder of Jews their official goal. Secretly, the Nazis planned to wipe out all the Jews in Europe.

Zofia Burowska's doll was saved for her by non-Jews. Zofia survived the Kraco ghetto in Poland and reclaimed her doll after the war.

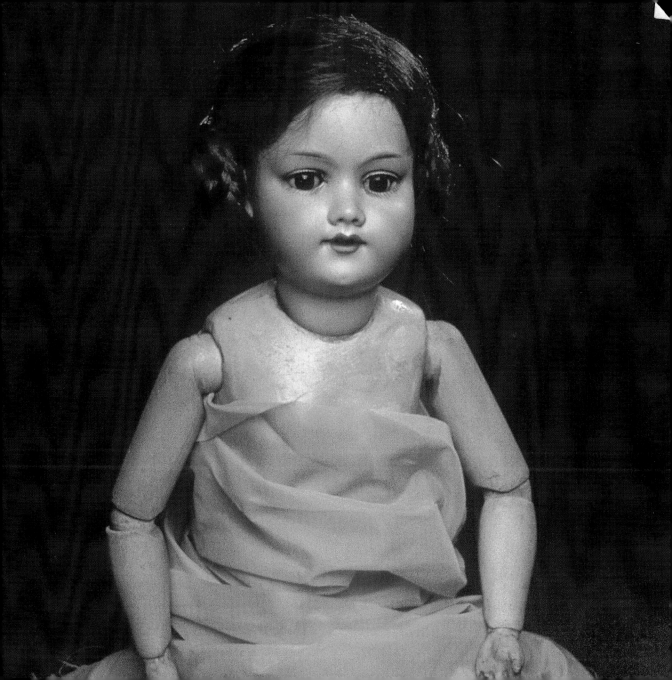

During the next 3 years, the Nazis murdered millions of Jewish people and others they felt were "inferior" or "sub-human." Their victims were shipped like cattle in boxcars. The trains rolled into towns such as Treblinka, Auschwitz, Dachau, and Buchenwald. There the Nazis built killing centers. The Nazis' victims were marched into closed rooms where they breathed poison gas. Their bodies were dumped into mass graves or burned.

By the war's end, about 2 of every 3 European Jews had been murdered. And along with those 6 million Jews, another 6 million "inferior" people of other groups had also been killed.

The three-floor Tower of Faces in the Museum's Permanent Exhibit is a collection of family photographs from one tiny Jewish town in Poland. A few of the townspeople survived the Holocaust, but their community vanished.

VISITING THE U.S. HOLOCAUST MEMORIAL MUSEUM

The Holocaust Museum has four floors with several different sections. Most sections are suggested for visitors 11 or older. Some areas on the first floor are recommended for visitors 8 and older.

The Permanent Exhibit is divided into 3 main parts, each taking 1 floor of the museum. "Nazi Assault" on the fourth floor covers the Nazi terror of 1933-1939.

Prisoners at Auschwitz made the original sign. This is a copy. It says, "Work Will Make Us Free." The letter "B" was purposely hung upside down, the prisoners' code for resistance.

19

The period 1940-1945 is covered in "The Final Solution" on the third floor. "Final Solution" was the Nazi term for making their murder of Jews legal.

The third section of the Permanent Exhibit is "Last Chapter." It deals with the people who helped resist the Nazis and the Holocaust **survivors'** (sur VIE verz) lives after the war.

The Hall of Remembrance on the second floor has an ever-burning flame in memory of Holocaust victims.

This photo shows the staircase and black granite wall (left) in the Hall of Witness at the Museum.

The first floor's Wall of Remembrance is a memorial to the approximately 1.5 million children murdered in the Holocaust. The first floor also has special, changing exhibitions.

The Wexner Learning Center in the museum allows people to find books, photos, and maps about the Holocaust. It also has recordings of survivors' stories.

The Meed Survivors' Registry in the Learning Center encourages people who lived under the Nazis to record their stories.

GLOSSARY

artifact (AHR teh fakt) — any product of a certain period in time or civilization

Holocaust (HAH luh kahst) — the planned mass murder of millions of people, especially Jews, by Nazi Germany during World War II

Nazi (NAHT see) — Adolph Hitler's ruling German political party (1933-1945), known for its brutal control of its subjects and the organized murder of millions

perish (PAIR ish) — to die

superior (soo PEER ee ur) — better than another; of very high quality

survivor (sur VIE ver) — one who lives or lasts through difficult events

INDEX

FURTHER READING

Find out more about the U.S. Holocaust Memorial Museum and the Holocaust in general with these helpful books and information sites:

Gold, Alison Leslie. *Memories of Anne Frank.* Scholastic, 1999.
Geier, Abraham. *Heroes of the Holocaust.* Berkley, 1998.

U.S. Holocaust Memorial Museum
   www.ushmm.org
U.S. Holocaust Memorial Museum Public Programs
   publicprograms@ushmm.org